Each Perfected Name

Each Perfected Name

Richard St. John

New Odyssey Series
Truman State University Press
Kirksville, Missouri

Copyright © 2015 Richard St. John
All rights reserved
tsup.truman.edu

Cover painting: *Akasha*, 2007 by Denise McMorrow Mahone. Reproduced with permission of the artist, www.denisemahone.com.

Cover design: Teresa Wheeler

Library of Congress Cataloging-in-Publication Data
St. John, Richard, 1952-
[Poems. Selections]
Each perfected name / Richard St. John.
        pages cm. — (New odyssey series)
ISBN 978-1-61248-130-2 (alk. paper) — ISBN 978-1-61248-131-9 (e-book)
I. Title.
PS3619.T249E33 2014
811'.6—dc23
                                                              2014016932

The paper in this publication meets or exceeds the minimum requirements of the American National Standard for Information Sciences—Permanence of Paper for Printed Library Materials, ANSI Z39.48–1992.

For Kate, again,
Wayne Peck, and
my sister, Barbara Lambdin

Contents

Acknowledgments

Many wonderful people have supported creation of this book, particularly members of my family, friends at Community House Presbyterian Church, and Pittsburgh's generous poetry community. They've shared the gifts of personal encouragement, artistic insight, candid feedback, opportunities to read, and other contributions likely beyond their knowing. I thank you all, named and unnamed here.

Among these many, Nancy Krygowski, Philip Terman, and Judith Vollmer contributed extraordinarily through warm and careful readings of full-length manuscript drafts, and in many other ways. Adrienne Block assisted with a generous final look.

For long-standing poetic support and comments on individual poems: Joan Bauer, Jay Carson, Peter Oresick, and Joseph Karasek.

For sustaining friendship and wisdom: Gary Govert, David Stasenko and Barbara Shema, Dave Beckwith, Keith Kuhn, Jon Lloyd, Urmi Ashar, Kathy Fox and other 2002 Loeb Fellows, James Stockard, Eve Beglarian, Peter Wright, Court Gould (thanks also for "commissioning" two of the poems in this book), Tina Calabro, Valentina Vavasis, Scott Young, Dave Brewton, Paul Tellers, Tirzah Mason, Steve Hollaway, Robert Hollander, Robert Wickenheiser, Claire Bateman, Gwen Ebert, Alfred Encarnacion, Rosaly DeMaios Roffman, Diane Kerr, Kelli Stevens Kane, Frank X. Gaspar, and the late Thomas Peer.

For their generous contributions of art and photography: Denise Mahone, Mark Perrott, and Jan Leo.

For reading opportunities and timely insight: Michael Wurster (thanks, too, for the anecdote that closes "Fireflies"), Michael Simms, Jan Beatty, Samuel Hazo, Erik Rosen, Arlene Weiner, Arlan Hess, Kathy Dorgan, Lisa Starr, Jisen Coghlan, Judith Robinson, and the Hemingway's Summer Reading Series team.

Deep thanks, of course, to the editors and staff at Truman

State University Press who believed in and brought to birth both of my full-length books.

Finally, there's the special troika who have most sustained me over the years: Kate St. John, Barbara Lambdin, and Wayne Peck.

Publication Credits

Special thanks to the editors and staff of the publications in which these poems previously appeared, sometimes in different versions.

Chautauqua: "Eclipse" and "Metaphysics of Thrushes."

5 a.m.: "'The Garden Will Come to You' / A Conversation" and "Lost Turtle."

The Fourth River: "A Blessing in Baltimore," "Pluto 1," "Pluto 2," and "Pluto 3." "Pluto 1" was reprinted in the magazine's online anthology celebrating the best work from its first ten issues.

New People: "Reading Shaw's Play *St. Joan*, at the Solstice, on a Greyhound, Heading Home," reprint.

Pittsburgh City Paper: "I Write to the G-20 Leaders in Advance of Their Pittsburgh Summit."

Pittsburgh City Paper online: "On Being Asked for a Poem That Embodies Non-Anthropocentric Spirituality."

Pittsburgh Post-Gazette: "Sparrow in the Supermarket."

Poet Lore: "The Sparrows of Bahrain."

Rune: "Vita Nuova."

St. Katherine Review: "Abhorrent Things."

Sustainable Pittsburgh online newsletter: "Reading Shaw's Play *St. Joan*, at the Solstice, on a Greyhound, Heading Home."

U.S. 1 Worksheets: "Penelope in Firelight."

I

Metaphysics of Thrushes

Leaving the bookstore, where I'd been skimming
Problem of the Soul, we turn past the T-shirt shops,
ice cream parlors, restaurants. No one is going
anywhere in particular. We pass
the doorway of a bar—a bright eddy of noise
swirls out and fades—then reach
some sleepy residential streets.

Suddenly, Kate stops. She cups her ears
and looks straight up. "Listen," she hushes.
I hear just . . . the autumn wind through treetops.
But she hops forward, three quick steps,
then stops again: "They're there!
The thrushes!" At last I hear
a tinny "*tzee . . . tzee . . . tzee.*"
She's running, almost dancing now, as if
to catch them high above—half a palm long,
mere fluff with mottled breasts. Flitting
through shadows, streetlight, in this quirky quest—
clapping with joy, and calling "sweethearts!"
and again, "my sweethearts!"—she is at her best.

From the sharp darkness, the thrushes call,
"*tzee . . . tzee . . .*" elusive, staticky;
in the streets below, almost unheard.
Night after night they make their distant way,
fragile, steadfast—leaning toward.

Second Birth

I would as lief pray with Kit Smart as with any man.
—Samuel Johnson

My mother is upstairs, in her bedroom crammed
with tracts and books on prayer. My sister
with Down syndrome is up there, too.
Their voices filter through the cheap construction.

Not words. It's mostly tone. Though I manage to hear,
"Motho' you *haf* to put tho' drops in yo' eyes . . ."
They go back and forth, a gusty wind, the intimate,
incomprehensible language of childhood twins.

Tonight, everything seems to be speaking
to my blindness and need: Her weekly pillbox,
its mornings and evenings making one day. That childish
cross-stitch of a lamb. Even our old cat, Kit Smart,

throws himself down on the fake flagstone flooring
beseeching me to pray: "*Mewp. Mewp,*" he says.
All I catch is tone. My mother and sister
are still going on. Twenty minutes, it's been—

no, really, fifty years, their shared laboring
converges, as our mom grows young again.
"This may seem a litto' strange," my sister told me
on the phone. "Sometimes we make animo' sounds."

"*Moo . . . moo. Baa . . . baa.*" The drops are still not in.
But the voices come through the thin drywall

less a dispute than a well-worn vaudeville act,
tendentious at times, yet they're clearly yucking it up.

"*Mewp . . . mewp*," says Kit Smart, his glowing eyes
at the foot of the sofa bed. "*Mewp . . . mewp*," I reply.

The Sparrows of Bahrain

Behind Beit Al Qur'an—its thirteen centuries of texts
enshrined in glass, where you can see beneath a lens
the holy verses on a grain of rice—the sparrows of Bahrain
scuffle by the trash bin, and leave
their delicate calligraphy upon the dust.

The price of oil goes up; they are not touched by it.
The causeway to the Saudi states shuts down;
the sparrows squabble, mate, and flutter on.
Communications towers, refineries, desalination schemes
are of another world to them.

In the twenty-seventh *sura* of Qur'an, Solomon has marshaled
all his *jinn*, his birds and men, into a vast battalion.
Sheba sends forth envoys bearing thick, tooled gold.
Solomon responds: "That which Allah has bestowed
on me is more than any wealth you send."

At the public dump in Manama, sparrows
move nimbly among the flames, finding
the tiny grains even the last few
poor within this oil emirate disdain.
On the final day, when darkness comes

and mountains pass away like clouds, when the last
oil spill has stained the last fair stretch
of sand, when the spreading desert

has engulfed the last hectare of working land,
when the gardens and the office towers have drained

the last sweet water flowing underground,
will the sparrows of Bahrain break into flame?
Will they become avenging angels?
Or only mark this desert place, like feeble
votive candles held against the dark?

Fireflies

Now it's July, the fireflies rise
from the feeble loam of our urban flower beds
and ill-kempt lawns. This could be
the ancient gnostic story—scattered sparks,
the trapped divine, floating up at last
to a higher place and time—except
that it happens now and here.

Where our neighbor's cat leaps at a pale green flame
and misses. Rorschach of black and white,
tiny as a kitten but on our block for years,
"Little One," her only name. "Little One,"
all of us purr as we stoop to nuzzle her
before she slips beneath a hedge or car.

Here where young kids jostle
in the tight-parked street. A long pass
wobbles, disappearing, spectral,
through a skein of phone lines, dark in the dusk,
then faintly silver in the dark.

Here where the One-Stop Oil Change
stays open late. Car in the arc lights,
on a lift. Shadow of a man

in overalls, moving in the pit.

Here at the weedy roadside, floating faces
of our Queen Anne's lace, tangled grapevine,
and a brace of foolish, orange lilies
that raise their trumpets to a streetlight
by the underpass. Among our holy oddities.

Where Stanley walks the double line
of Cranston Boulevard. The great machines
blast past. No use dialing 911. Pointless, too,
to talk with him—as he bows deeply,
sweeping out one arm, pausing, then the other one,
catching the glowing headlights on his palms.

Helsinki Accord

For Erkki, Helena, and Irja Mäkinen

       The air swept clean
by long July light, the light
powdery gravel on the path,
the silver and green leaves
washing above.

       Here in Helsinki
I've been learning to count again.
"Ook-si" "Kok-si" "Kolemen."
To say "dog" and "cat."
Meeting a mother like
and yet unlike my own—
stouter, and with a face
more round.

       Maybe it takes
the sieve of a foreign language
to simplify and clean.
Maybe it takes the silence
of seven winter months,
the heavy stones of dark.

       I tell myself
that I can keep this intimate
accord, written though it is
on fragile, parchment light.

But don't we always
break these vows?
The promise of morning.
The high blue dome
of noon. The bread
of clouds. The shallow cup
worn in a granite step.

Still, I open up
the wrapper from a pastry,
boiled egg and butter,
salt not sweet, and unfold
it on this weathered bench,
preparing even now
to break and eat.

Penelope in Firelight (I)

In all of his marvelous journeys
he'd never seen anything like it: the tree
that had rooted their marriage bed was gone
into autumn. He watched her for hours

sewing in the firelight, her still-lovely limbs
bare and moving gracefully; an effortless
assurance and letting-go that spread a tapestry
of yellows, duns, and browns evenly at her feet.

These nights, when she turned from him in bed,
she meant nothing by it. A natural thing—the way
that fall comes on, and then, the hard, sharp
sting of snow. She knew as well as he did

that Circe and Calypso were only emblems of desire
that still burned on in him. That's why he'd come home.
That's why he studies her so closely now. That's why
the slender, silvery needle, on which she lavishes

her easy, whole-hearted attention, terrifies him
as nothing on the fields of Ilium had ever done.

The Moon, the Stars, the Missing Mass

For Keith Kuhn, in memory of his son

Above: the merest hairline fracture of a moon. Beyond:
the cold, cracked glass, the terrible non-pattern
of the stars. Somewhere among: the sudden, wheeling
absence of your son. Wafer-thin dimensions. Weightless quarks.
Spooky action at a distance. Odd entanglements.

You're playing Bach in total darkness. Ice whispers
in the cold cloud-chamber of your whiskey glass, leaving
its afterimage in the varnish, pale nebula, indelible white ring.
Sip of whiskey. Black keys, white keys. Whisperings.

Spooky action at a distance, this haunting counterpoint
across so many years. *Down. Up. Bottom. Top.*
Strange. Charm. Whiskey and cold glass. Ninety percent of mass
is somewhere else. Call it dark matter, unearthly

gravitas. *Up. Down. Strange. Charm.* Love,
that cannot change a thing. Reverberations, resonance.
Cold as whiskey's fire. Indelible, ineffable
as Bach, yet heavy as an ache. Filling the unseen
fractures, fissures, everywhere.

Sparrow in the Supermarket

His wings flail
fast as his heart.

It is light
then it is dark.

There is an aisle of bread
if he could see it.

There is another sparrow
or does he dream it?

It makes no sound.
It never rests.

There is a lovely
black spot on its breast.

At the mirror
in every row

they meet
and bow.

It mimics
his each move.

There is a low hard sky
he cannot get above.

The Virtue That Makes All Others Possible

Before he disappeared forever, before his lone, obsessive music
sent him forth, a man who'd knelt each spring, in the big
corner garden of their city lot, digging in a thousand bulbs, jonquils
and daffodils—just before—he left his wife of fifty years
a sandwich, cut on the diagonal, and some days I'm tempted
to leave like that, two neat triangles on the kitchen plate, elegant
little flags of surrender, small sails to travel somewhere else,
the gentle self-effacement of it, the decency,

                               and of course
its utter indecency, the knife across the bread, the cruel
angularity of it, the huge half-lie of it, the tidy triangular note
of it, as if to say *I was the caring one, you were the one
who never cared enough*, leaving the left-ones stunned and angry
and bereft, all for a lack of courage, or thin stash of courage
finally played out, courage, the virtue, Aristotle tells us, that makes
all other virtues possible, but while we were waiting, stunned
and guessing *was he lost or had he died?* we walked the trails
of the city parks, waited by the homeless shelters, where
I did my stint, sitting on a concrete block, off from the entrance,
close enough to watch, well before the food line formed, people
only drifting in and out and saying "hi" to Manny, dark skinned
in a blue-striped rugby shirt, white Capri pants and—no lie—
some kind of sailor's cap, who pranced and posed as anyone
came up, charming and fierce by turns, acting each turn
poised and self-possessed: "You'd better *not* drop a crate of fruit
on *my* foot again . . ." and cadging everyone for just a dollar,
for some ice cream, from the ice cream truck,

                               Manny, a character,

focus of the scene, focused on one thing, and who can blame him?
who *doesn't* want something sweet, after all? I thought
how, for me, one dollar is nothing, a hundred doesn't hurt, yet
for him, it is this whole afternoon's obsession, its riff, its music,
but when Aristotle says "character," says "acting," he means
something like habit, over time becoming solid, the way an old man
might make a sandwich, then put away the cutting board,
sweep up the crumbs and leave the counter clean,

                                        a life
of virtuous choosing, Aristotle's image, the classical charioteer
holding the surging reins, mastering the horses of his soul, neither
depressed nor ebullient, as Aristotle's student Alexander, who
never paid attention but surely had courage, sweeping across Asia
with his chariots, his disciplined army, bogged down admittedly
in the rough terrain of Turkistan, Afghanistan, yet
bravely coming through with Indus at his feet,

                                oh, how I hate
and envy Aristotle, his duty and his golden mean, his heavy
successors, too, *The Consolation* of Boethius, warning
of Fortune's circus wheel with its carnival music,
which gives and takes in random fate, no consolation really,
just a grim admonition to tough it out, it seems to me,
but Manny's still prancing and cadging for his dollar, as
the daffodils and jonquils will surely prance and pose next spring
beautiful and ebullient,

                        and now I regret I didn't give him a dollar
for all the usual reasons: intruding on his space, fearing
to condescend, *what would he do with it after all?* and only twenties
in my wallet, I regret, my own poor stack of courage now played out,
regret I didn't take a twenty and lay it, thin and damp across
the pale, open triangle of his palm, for now I feel he might

have given *me* something too, but instead the ice cream truck pulled up, and paused, but didn't stop, leaving that terrible, tinny, mechanical music that—will as I might—I can't get out of my head.

Irrefutable Logic of the Tiles

For Rick Lowe

Yet my good friend's life was saved by Aristotle
and his disciple Arthur, who taught from memory
the *Logic* and the *Ethics* in a burned-out Houston warehouse,
among the flattened cardboard boxes and piles of crumpled clothes,
hands twitching from the vodka and amphetamines, and Rick,
no books in his own home either, would sneak into the library
to check, finding that Arthur had it right, down to the nuance
and the numbered line, though Arthur also disappeared
leaving behind the cardboard pallet and the clothes,
and troubling doubts about entelechy and power of the mind.

* * *

The bright immutable tiles of the stars
aren't yet out over Houston, only twilit August sky
above the liquor billboards and the vacant lots,
over the generous urban acre Rick has helped rebuild:
a row of shotgun houses and a juke joint down the block
restored; breezy cottonwoods; the crunch of limestone gravel
in the shared backyards. On one wooden stoop
Rick and three old friends crack jokes and calculate
in multiples of five. The slap of dominoes, the hard,
irrefutable logic of the tiles—brute chance or fate
of five and twenty, fifteen, five—Arthur's old lessons
in memory, the stoic virtues, and stern choice.

* * *

But that's not the feel of it, each small tally
adding to the "house" of scores, as the unforgiving sun
goes down, evening's coolness settles on.
Rick is forced to knock. "Ella, Stella, Della!"
Johnson calls. The easy clink and click
as they create another day's odd, fragile shape
from the bone pile. It takes a special eye to see beyond
the streetlights, but overhead now, reappear
the fiery, courageous, twitchy little stars,
and no one seems to care if they're divisible by five.

〱

II

Eclipse

Tonight, but later, comes the moon's eclipse. Now,
on the lake, the cataract of ice has softened at its edge.
Water runs in the swales of cul-de-sacs. Along the damp
dark passageways through last year's leaves, this spring's voles
move silently. Now, the owls in the spare and moonlit trees
scan the dim terrain to listen, turn the smooth uncanny
pivot of each disk-like face, each pale Janus mask.

My mother sleeps. She sleeps more and more these days.
Bent to a C even when she stands, C of Contentment,
Children grown, her half-hemisphere of porous, brittle bones.
Sleeping more and hearing less, little loops of recurrence
in her speech. This visit home, her grayish look
through cataracts, of being somewhere else. Some dim force
pulls her to the edge of conversations. Who can guess?

Through the moon-wash floats a family of deer,
finding moss that only yesterday was snow.
Bats make their wobbly first maneuvers
from their eaves. Sap must be rising, insects out
invisible to me. The air, so warm this afternoon,
rings sharp and clear. Tap it, you can almost see
reverberations ripple outward, resonate and disappear.

We're here for her grandchild's baby shower; she sleeps, too,
more tired than usual. Stretched on the sofa. Lamp still on,
casting its luminescent calm. Yet the girl's restless:
Backache. Blood-flushed cheek. She flicks away

a dampened tendril of her hair. Turns again to ease
the C-sway of her spine. Turns, so now the lightfall
leaves its glow across her belly's globe, shadow on her arm.

Geese overhead, passing somewhere else. Now the disk of moon
drags the tides along, pulled in turn by the stirring earth.
Now its leading edge is overtaken by a wedge of dark
until, in our penumbra, it turns blood red, then
black again. We shiver as we watch—not a disappearance
but a giving place—hold our breath, waiting
for the thin, bright crescent to emerge.

Vita Nuova

For weeks I lay
in the bright box.
No one touched me much.

Around me, sweet, thick oxygen
probed my still-squinched eyes
and fed my tiny lungs.

My mother must have stood beyond
thick glass; she couldn't do a thing
but pray and watch my plight.

It was the beginning
of my blindness and my need.
The start of my new life.

Succinct Meditations on Fire

*Two things fill the mind with ever new and
increasing admiration and reverence [. . .]: the
starry heavens above me and the moral law
within me.*

—Immanuel Kant

Kant, my tepid brother, pale
as me. He loved his name,
Immanuel, and claimed to see
God with us in the starry
lineaments of reason
pin-pricked across Man's mind.
Pure, fixed lights
of freedom, moral obligation—
"without which the brutes fly blind."

* * *

At thirty-two,
he nearly proposed
to a lithe Westphalian girl.

Numbered the silver moons
spread out across a dark
felt tablecloth. A single candle
flickered in his rooms.
Enough? Again and again,
he counts the coins.

* * *

Meanwhile, her carriage
thundered through the heath.
Snowdrops, silver in her hair,
flashed in the coach-light,
melted off. Outside,
the crystal air. The night. The great
dark horses and their steaming breath.

* * *

Fifty now, he makes up maxims:
"Never marry." "Smoke one pipe per day."
Working routine shifts, he's tunneling
his moral *Groundwork*. A whole
so cool, so categorical, refined,
its paths so labyrinthine, ever
deeper in the mind. Keen-eyed mole
in search of something absolutely sure,
he follows the flicker of a silver seam,
forgetting that the constellations begin in fire.

Lost Turtle

Answers to "Beatrice"
Last seen on Bellerock Place
Reward Offered $$ Thanks
        —Flier on a neighborhood telephone pole

We're all looking for her.
        And it's good
there's a reward
        because we've read
we have to pass through flame
        to reach her.

Beatrice! What are you doing
        in that mundane shell,
plodding around
        like the rest of us?

This isn't the Earthly Paradise.
        Bellerock Place
is an urban street
        parked to the max with cars.
Our dogs are cunning
        and fierce, and after midnight
packs of city rats get desperate.

We're all frantic
        to find her
in our gardens
        and small backyards.

In the waning light,
	I keep staring at
that mottled rock
	by our crushed
aluminum downspout.

Now it appears
	the tiniest tilt of the head
is all it takes.
	She's here! She's
always been right here.
	Under our drooping rosebush,
come out to see the stars.

"Dog Days" / A Conversation

When you look behind the stars, there are more stars.
—Frank X. Gaspar

You're right, of course, behind the mystery
of the universe is the mystery of ourselves,
trying to make sense of things. But the sad fact is
I can't see the stars. They let me skip the quiz
on constellations, as a kid in Boy Scouts.
Just as, in gym class, I jumped incredibly
from a C to a B the semester I sat out
with an eye injury. They did, however, insist
I watch the movies in Drivers Ed., where I learned—
as a young girl stamped the brakes, and everything
flew forward in the car, even her flowing hair—
*In an accident, books can become
instruments of destruction.* Something you must
have found from your own religious reading. All this,
without a prayer I'd ever drive: *Unsafe at any speed*,
as Ralph Nader described the '63 Corvairs
bursting into flame. Leaving me even today
in childish mystification—as everywhere
adults, without a thought, do all the things
I've never done: never had a child; unable to install
the simplest wiring; paying someone else
to add the kitchen sunroom to my house.
Am I too sheltered, still? Oblivious
to the great fires wheeling above, the lightning
hidden in my walls, the son or daughter
blurring from birth to seventh grade? I wonder,
as I watch the Lady with Three Dogs,

our neighborhood's Holy Fool, passing
in the alley just behind our house. "The Man
with the Beautiful Kitchen," she called me once.
It's only fair, I guess, because that's where I sit
as Sirius, you tell me, begins to rise
mysteriously, this August night, so far above
my comfortable chair. The plain oak table.
Rothko poster floating on the wall. The clean
white cabinets, their glowing golden knobs.
Just the sort of kitchen a real adult ought to have.

Odysseus Alone (II)

Each day they weave their lives
more beautifully together, threads
of care and conversation. The tiny tearings
and mendings that make any marriage.

Firstlight and firelight: quick kiss,
a hug, a kindly touch. Everything she has
and not enough. These nights, he lies in silence,
tensed. As if he's back in the sullen belly

of the wooden horse—but, now, alone.
The trapdoor creaks. Armored and enraged,
he prowls the streets and opens every door.
He seeks and seeks—but there's no enemy

to slay or servant girl to rape. Just cool silence.
Blind corridors and empty vestibules,
torchlight, heavy tapestries, the ivory altars
of the household gods. Last, an echoing room:

agéd Priam and pale Hecuba,
a half-filled bowl of fruit, a plate of fish,
a glinting flask of wine. His feet won't move.
His hand won't raise his sword. That's always when

Penelope wakes him with a gentle kiss.
Even the great Odysseus can't unravel this.

The Wolf at Gubbio

We all want Saint Francis to come
and rescue our little town.
I'm trying, now, to bless that Francis
won't arrive: the wolf still roams,
ravenous as ever.

                Not just in our dreams
but carrying off a cousin or a friend.
Present, too, in posses we routinely send
into the dark with torches, clubs, and chains.
They do it out of hunger.

                            Hunger
remains—loping through
the shaggy evergreens, dragging
the lengthened shadow of its need.

But, these days, townsfolk also
talk with each other more, gathered
at the well, or over bread, even
at the funerals.

                  Becoming, over years,
a part of what makes Gubbio
Gubbio, it is said.

Prom Night

Anybody else would call it innocent:
this starry girl and gangly boy on the deck
of the Gateway Partyliner. He's wearing
his father's out-of-style dinner jacket.
She's in a short white dress. They've just escaped
the too-loud band, the cooling rigatoni
in its silver bins. They stand at the rail,
silent for a time, as a chill wind scuffs
the wavering lights on the passing Allegheny.

It's really the scene of a crime: how, when
she leans to him with the softest little pout
and says "it's cold tonight," he doesn't respond,
except with a stiff, obligatory arm
across her shoulder. I'd like to believe
it's someone else who makes that awful cut
through her dream of what the evening should have been.
But on the grainy surveillance tape of memory
it's clearly me, acting from some churchy fear
of taking things "too far." And that's only one item
on my long rap-sheet of adolescent cruelties.

Yet, if I could go back—to that bad sound track
of "Hey Jude"; to the pallid, heart-sized slabs
of rare prime rib under their orange lamp;
to the mesmerizing churn of the paddle wheel
pushing the lights of the river ever behind us—
I don't see how I could undo the thing

without some new entanglement.
All I can do, I guess, is bless that girl
with her eager upturned face. And if I have to bless
that prissy fool, lost in his stiff, white,
oversized jacket, maybe that's o.k., too.

Pluto 1

It was a schoolgirl who named Pluto, her entry picked
because the god could make himself invisible. I like that
for its reticence. I like to see the underworld
not as a dreary place of death, but as a school
of mortal limits, where even Eurydice has merely
the beauty of the girl next door, her long red hair
flown frizzed across her shoulders. She listens to Persephone
describe her husband's gift, the cut red facets
of the seeds, which even in the sullen light, gave off
an ember's radiance. And where, though Orpheus *wishes*
for the genius to entrance the very stones and trees,
he's just another singer from a punk garage band
who always follows her around. This afternoon
I'm watching the school guard, in her chartreuse vest, blue cap,
who stops the traffic outside Martin Luther King, who helps
the children crossing to the other side, who sets her white-gloved
    hand
on the shoulder of a sobbing girl (red plastic beads
are glowing in her shaking braids), a girl who might have
submitted "Rhinestone," one of the many names that didn't win.

Faithfulness (III)

She taught him with her weaving, over time,
to view her with beloved detachment, a thing
growing seamlessly, a beautiful pattern
subdued in color. He'd been promised peace

and here it was. He'd faithfully obeyed
the charge he'd heard from wise Tiresias
deep in the underworld: On reaching home,
to leave the sea—carrying his oar so far

a passerby who'd never seen the shore
would comment on the curious winnowing fan
he shouldered. There, he'd made his sacrifice
of honey and milk, barley, and sweet wine.

Yet, watching her innocent sleep, he longs for more,
even if it sends him, madly, sailing off the earth.

Inner Ear

He was an old dog, Einstein, gradually going blind,
already "deaf as a post." They found him one night
turning inexplicably, in useless, lurching circles.
My good friend recalls lifting him into the car;
the musk of his dampened Airedale fur. But it
wasn't a stroke, something rather, with his inner ear.
In only a week, he was back to his normal
halting walk, though with an unaccustomed,
gentle look, as if he could hear again,
but listened to something far beyond them now.

"O, the Lord is subtle . . . subtle . . ." —Einstein
at a blackboard, chalked with dense equations.
I'm thinking of this on an aimless, circling walk,
thinking of Wordsworth, too. Wondering if
it matters that, one moonlit night, he steals
a rowboat tied to a willow tree, then rows
with adolescent hubris toward a far, fixed point.
Suddenly, *a huge peak, black and huge . . .*
rises in his sight, strides after him, and turns him back,
leaving just *a dim and undetermined sense*
of unknown modes of being. . . . That's when

from the rolled-down window of a slate-gray SUV
a man leans out. His wife in a sari.
"The tunnel . . . it is blocked . . . entirely. . . ." They need
directions, not poor Wordsworth turning round his boat.
So I talk them through a route. Yet, however practical

their plea, they're looking for the Hindu temple, its tower
a ziggurat, glowing gold and white above the interstate,
a realm of deities unknown to me. I find one in a book

who on his journey toward enlightenment is told
he cannot bring his old dog with him, too. The faithful beast
looks up from licking at his cracked and bleeding paws,
and cocks his ears. Yudhisthira ponders seven days,
then picks his way as he descends the mountain path
with Dharma limping at his side. But now,
the craggy landscape's different, as if the whole
supporting universe had been, ever so subtly, bent.

III

December, New Millennium

So warm, the hedges almost bloom, though the jagged skeletons
of fake, electric icicles are twined along a front-yard chain-link
    fence.
In the windows, faded Steelers signs, tribal gear still out
although the season's done. Lazy, from the playground, comes
the *pock . . . pock . . . pock* and *thunk* of basketball. And on the
    bus today,
a man, almost theatrical, in calf-high boots and cape, was reading
a garden book: bright pink and purple squares—laurels,
    rhododendrons—
species being forced beyond this climate zone. Yet for us, it's
this kiss of almost summer, fragrant with transience and sun.
It's like magic: the air so breathy, we pretend
our leisurely earth is washing itself again. Though, in the end,
magic will not save us, cape and wand, rituals and signs, potions,
costly powders, tusks and bones, procured from tawdry
dealers in such things, shark fins, albino skin, rhinoceros horn.

Abhorrent Things

*You shall not eat any abhorrent thing. . . . of those
that chew the cud or have the hoof cleft you shall
not eat these: the camel, the hare, and the rock bad-
ger, because they chew the cud but do not divide the
hoof; they are unclean for you. And the pig, because
it divides the hoof but does not chew the cud, is
unclean for you. You shall not eat their meat, and
you shall not touch their carcasses.*
—Deuteronomy 14:3–8

There's the pig, of course,
with its cloven hoof
and its failure
to ruminate, eating the slops
but not reconsidering—
over and over—
insufficiently Talmudic.

Why, though, the camel?
Bearer of so many burdens,
considering as he walks.

And the hare:
thinking and thinking
as it nibbles the pale grass?

But my heart goes out
to the rock badger.
Fierce in its independent
ruminations. It was a badger,
I think, we struck on I-80—

no—grazed, dazed. We watched
it lumber into the swale,
then up and off.

We never saw it again.
Maybe it lived
a long, abhorrent life
among the roots and shaley rocks
of northern Pennsylvania.

Maybe God, too, reconsidered
and, at last, as shadows
lengthened into dusk,
gathered the forbidden carcass
into the open, cloven
parting of his arms.

Pluto 2

*After the action of the International Astronomers Union
(8/24/06)*

Poor Pluto, icy stone, never so lovely as Venus
or possessing Jupiter's pull. Dragging along
your equal moon, that old cold pagan dance-partner,
Charon. Still tangled up with Neptune's elliptic
and its inner tides. Second-tier, our mirror,
unable even to clear your wobbly orbit of debris.
Yet, for all of it, the sun's faint ray still falls
on your gravelly eye.   A great debate—and bang!—
you're X'ed from the canon by the IAU, in Prague
not Rome, but still the same: too many minor objects
threatening the cosmic balance. It's just as Irenaeus
argued and the holy fathers, in their wisdom, then declared
the gnostic gospels bogus—full of outlandish sayings
like: "Pick up a stone, and you will find me there."

Learning with the Lost

For Robert Hollander—celebrating 40 years as professor
of European literature

Great teachers teach us nothing. At best they love
their subject deeply, and we take
a bit of that away. You taught us Dante: On a dike above

a burning plain, he peers at the charred and upturned face
of his own teacher, but the face I see is yours.
Around us now, the broad white flakes

of flame are falling like hot phosphorous
and I wonder what you're doing here—
wherever here is—tanned and vigorous,

not like a shade at all. Perhaps because it's queer
that anyone could love a poem so much,
an immoderate passion for these forty years.

There was other work to do, after all. Ride any bus
through Kinshasa. Nothing to buy
at the corrugated market stalls. Pale gray dust

on the street kids at the corner. The one dull eye
of a three-legged dog. Everywhere grief
settles on the unprotected, like ashes from the sky.

* * *

And yet, head bowed, I thank you, even for the brief
treasure of a long-past, one-semester course,
the customary green of Dante's laurel wreath

a hope that beauty begets beauty, the fair calls forth
some symmetry of fairness in our hearts. You run,
driven now across the plain, giving it all you're worth

not, as Dante says, *like one who lost, but one who won.*
But is it that easy? Can we forgive
the poet, who—for all the affection

that he shows Brunetto and the sodomites adrift
in the seventh circle—still he has them damned
and, in the poem, slips the added shiv

of outing them? By our forgiveness stand
aside while fire falls on others? Cut to the plain
outside of Sodom. There we find Abraham

bargaining with God. *Would the Lord refrain*
from destroying the city for fifty just men?
What of forty-five? Would God inflict such pain

if only short a few? . . . And so on, down to ten.
Even God learns, it seems, and learns through us.
For though the fire fell, there's a story where he bends

to ponder—and this is mysterious
to all the others, watching with their stones—
then writes with his finger in the warm gray dust.

* * *

Poets stranded on a narrow dike, like the ones
built of stone to guard their cities from the sea or floods
by the cautious Flemings and the Paduans.

The broad white flakes are falling. Only the blood
boiling in the fosse—its vapor—shields us overhead.
Distant puffs of sand appear, and grow in magnitude

until a troop of winded, blackened shades
comes up beside. One of them looks hard
at us, squinting like a tailor at his thread

eager to mend some tear or flaw. His marred
features swim before us, they fill the space
around us now, a circle widening. He reaches toward

us with his eyes. We meet the rapt face
of this naked man, unnamed and disapproved,
and—in the moment we return that gaze—
what we learn, and learn again, is love.

A Blessing in Baltimore

You must take another way. . . .

—*Inferno* I, 93

The old South Boston Aquarium stands
in a Sahara of snow now.

—"For the Union Dead"

The seventh apartment was closely shrouded in black
velvet tapestries. . . .

—"The Masque of the Red Death"

Tomorrow, following the christening
of your adopted son, I'll take some time
to see the National Aquarium.
I'm writing this because a poem
is all I have by way of gift
and I find that what I mean to write
isn't just about your sudden life
as parents of a multiracial son,
but about the Baltimore—as place, yet more
than place—that you'll be living in.

Each time I come

I watch the fish spin round and round
the great, illuminated, multistory tank.
Silver and gray-green, like currency in wind,
they flicker, each according to its kind.
Sea bass, mackerel, and halibut,
they speed and spiral: Ceaseless. Sleepless.
Oblivious. Intent. Outside, the buses
idle at the curb. Reboarding visitors
recall the banners, glass pavilion shops and food
of festive, redeveloped Baltimore. It's sad,

a kind of spiral in: how people mill around
this tidy city built for them to see,
less like a city than a mall back home,
and still believe in it, don't find it false
or feel some loss.
                          In contrast, your adoption was
a movement outward: legal papers
and your signature, a costly, wavering blue line
deployed in ordinary ballpoint pen,
recorded with the deeds at Houston's courthouse,
while you stepped out, an infant at your arms,
into that huge and foreign sky, its great
piled waterstacks of cloud, so open and so high.

To visit you we cross Antietam Creek.
Pale companies of leaves plaster the water
and drift to the Potomac, past the battlefields
where both sides lost. They dapple
the entry porticos of gated towns
and sprinkle the swing sets and fall upon
a child's sneaker in a private lawn.
They flicker like a dream among
the mortgage tax–deductions and the infrastructure bonds.
They gather in the swales along the interstates
and by the wheelstops in the shopping center lots.
They spiral through the subdivided farmlands
that the Army of Northern Virginia
could not save. Then, at last, float down
to segregated Washington.
                          We drive on
through failing twilight into Baltimore.

Baltimore, that border town and sometime home
to Douglass, Poe, and Key. Even from a distance
we can see the halo over Camden Yards.
The Orioles have won again, it seems, and as we drive
the post-game fireworks appear—to us
like brittle, shattering chrysanthemums,
but to the ticket-holders in the stands
like overarching and fantastic rooms
of blue, then purple, green, orange, white and violet
and then—*b-bang-b-bang bang-boom*—
a room of black. I imagine all those human faces
looking up. Then the ghostly crowd, the parking lot
(Black street kids rove among the rows of cars),
the doors unlocking and the keys, the silent engines
flaring up and driving home. The smoke—
like one of Poe's uneasy dreams—descends
upon the darkened and divided town.

Tomorrow, at a polished and ornate
baptismal font, you'll set apart your son
from all the principalities and powers of dark.
But there, in the sunny transept, with the flowers,
with the stolid congregation dressed to please,
where the rector dips his thumb and makes
the watery mark on Gibson's forehead, the powers
are gathered in the room. It's not that vestments
or the people in their suits and floral prints
are bad. Yet they can form a narrow circle
like the font's dark wood—a circumscription
savage, harsh, and dense, and filled with temptations
to protect and shield.

So, what can I
who haven't come so far or risked as much,
possibly say to you, to guide or bless?
I'll give you only my imagined picture
of a place. There, women lean across
the fences of the tiny yards—to mark a union
or to mourn a loss. Their small, unconsecrated plots
enclose some beaten soil, a strip of vegetables
or, maybe, blue forget-me-nots. A tap runs.
And, through the humid evening air, you hear
the dishes sloshing in a sink next door.
On summer afternoons, the neighborhood cascades
down low front stoops, along the baking rowhouse block.
A small patrol of dogs sniffs trash. And children
chase each other on the street and walks.
Someone with a wrench has turned a hydrant open
and the kids converge. The shirts and shoes fly off.
The water froths—anarchic and impure
and shared—and all the taxpayers' money
overflows the gutters and the broken curbs.

Triple Fence at Friendship Park, California

You could crawl through the old fence.
Then, only a hand.
Now just fingertips can touch.

Maria's Song

An old story: the girl was pregnant, had spent
the night on the streets of Washington. It looked like
she'd come for a green card, or maybe to get warm

and to sneak our office bathroom. We never do this,
but I let her in. "I'm here to see my aunt, she works
to keep clean this building." "They're only here at night,"

I explained. But there was something luminous
about her. Even the congressman saw it
as he passed through. She was crying, then,

but when she calmed, we sent her down
with an aide and pass to peek for a moment
into the chambers. But she didn't stop at the parted door—

she must have seen her aunt, cleaning something spilled
in the west aisle, and who could've guessed, the timid girl
barreled right in, with a host of House guards

scurrying behind; they paused, though—the human
weight of it—as the two embraced. That's when, I'm told,
the girl broke into her crazed and terrifying song.

Argos (IV)

How had he looked to her when he'd come home?
He didn't know, what with the way the gods
were forever cloaking men in mist, giving the old
a youthful glow. He wasn't even sure

what he'd hoped of her after all those years—
but likely more than any mortal woman
could bestow. He had reached his household gates
at dusk, blind with rage and longing. Even now,

he can't shake off the sour smell of his beggar's shawl.
Watching her easy gestures by the fire, he still
carries a small, rag bundle of resentments.
He recalls, again, the hour he returned:

his old dog, Argos, dim-eyed and deaf,
had struggled to rise from his bed of refuse
and debris, and wagged his palsied tail
in recognition. That's when the brave Odysseus

had shed a single, ignorant tear.
Only old Argos saw things as they are.

I Write to the G-20 Leaders in Advance of Their Pittsburgh Summit

> *At the end of the appointed time, I, Nebuchadnezzar*
> *raised my eyes to heaven and I returned to my right*
> *mind.*
>
> —Daniel 4:34

We are all tethered to an iron ring.
We have all been eating grass,
dreaming uneasy dreams. All
of us crazed, all cut off.

When I look into the face
of Blake's *Nebuchadnezzar*, I see
my own slack mouth, dazed eyes—
perplexed, distracted, terrified.

But it's you I want to speak with. You,
after all, strolled through the hanging gardens,
paused on the palace roof to admire the view,
savored November oranges
while scanning the morning's briefing book.

Though we all bowed down, you called
for the sound of timbrel, zither, pipe, and horn.
Furnace that had to burn, that glowed like gold.
Everything yearned around it like the sun.

Each day, we came again
with something: bundle of brushwood
on our backs; cool melon on a silver tray;

a briefing book, composed in our own
exquisite hand, in the learnèd
immortal language of Babylon.

* * *

Thanks for your response. Too bad
you can't take time to meet me here.
We might have talked about Blake,
who saw God's living fire

in *minúte particulars*. Say, a single grain
of limestone from the trail that runs
past our high-rise jail. Pale
as a fleck of bone from a crematorium;

to Blake, an open door, a stone
rolled from an empty sepulcher. Or, say,
the muffled sound of jostling men, the squeak of shoes
from an unseen, hardwood floor. Or a man alone

in a small, hot room. He spreads a frayed
gray prison bath towel out in front of him
and leans toward Mecca once again. Or, say,
a girl in the simplest black dress and polished shoes,

who stands in a parking lot and gazes up
toward a small, wired window on the highest floor.
Her hair in beaded braids, she lifts her arms
halfway, as if to fly, but can't—and stays.

* * *

Let's talk about fear.
That starry void
of death and finitude—
the way it spreads from us
in rings. All your textbooks
start with that, the cold
abstraction of scarcity.
From that they build.
A ring of iron; the solid stone
of barn; or cairn; or Stonehenge;
battle-hard patrols of soldiers
moving out; rings of the Gobi Desert
spreading south.

Blake starts somewhere else:
that minute grain of sand,
a fleck of fire, a star
turned inside out, a woman
gazing upwards
from a parking lot.

*Five windows light
the cavern'd Man:
thro' one he breathes the air;
Thro' one hears music
of the spheres; . . . thro' one can look
And see small portions
of the Eternal World.*

* * *

You've been having dreams
no one can interpret:

Strapped to a gurney, moving fast
along a sterile corridor.

Metal ventilator for a lung
linked to a furnace by an iron chain.

Counting every heartbeat,
16 . . . 18 . . . 20 . . . they appear

flattened into numbers
on the monitor. 30 . . . 34 . . .

Your heart is clanking now.
Your doctors nod.

Black hydra of a catheter.
Then this: outside of Lagos

in a field stripped bare
of everything but pipeline,

a kid in a "No Fear" T-shirt
and torn shoes—

bending his knees
and breathing fumes—

scoops tapped gasoline
into a rusty can. Then

the scene bursts into flame.

* * *

Don't claim
you haven't been warned.
Every minute particular
is saying something.

Scribble on the sidewalk
in a child's chalk.
Tagging that city workers
have been scraping off
the walls of our convention center hall.
Whatever some young Billy Blake
might be etching on his protest sign:

> *He who binds to himself a joy*
> *Does the winged life destroy.*

—

> *In every Infant's cry of fear,*
> *. . . The mind-forg'd manacles I hear.*

Of course it's inscrutable,
written in reverse
on copper plate, as in a mirror,

waiting for the bite of vinegar
and salt armoniac, the ghostly wash
of aqua fortis, to appear.

No one in your position
has time, of course,
for so much detail. You'll
soon be taking off, doing your best
in preparation on the eight-hour flight:
drafts of speeches; close advisors
handing you their latest brief
on macroeconomics; a moment
stolen to call your wife.

Still, here's my advice
for the opening banquet:
I love the beauty
of a silver chafing dish,
the delicate curve
of crystal, too. They could be
the serving vessels
to the hidden, holy ark
in any human heart. But when
the waiter passes you
a hand-tooled copper plate—
the flash of a wrist,
a mark you glimpse
beneath a starched white sleeve,
ask him about it. Tattoo? Or scar?

Maybe it's a Star of David.
Or, if he's very old, a number
in blue, a faded ghost.
There must be a story behind it.
Maybe it's a saber? Or a rose?
Or the pans of justice and crude scale?

* * *

What if finitude
is like an open field,
a small one,
where a king, who's lost
his mind, is tethered, on all fours,
feeding among the bunchgrass,
lilies, and the mustard seed,
his tangled hair
matted with burdock,
drenched with dew?

What if he wipes his eyes
and what had seemed a starry void
becomes a single evening,
twilight, by a riverside?

Two stars seem to rise
above the 10th Street Bridge.
Mallards putter in the weeds
around a half-sunk barge.

It's September, soon
they'll be gone from us.
Even the one
who tarries in his flight
to snag a last lucky crust
from the oily surface
of the Mon, even that one
is a *world of delight*.

Reading Shaw's Play *St. Joan*, at the Solstice, on a Greyhound, Heading Home

The year comes round again, with its own dark
fairness. Out on the turnpike, flecks of sleet.
Lightning through night clouds, ghostly, then stark.
Echo of thunder. In the tabloid at my seat
old scatterings return:
flicker of war in the Congo and Sudan,
late-season hurricanes, tainted meat.

All around me, whispered conversations of the poor.
Two rows up, a solitary reading lamp.
We're making good time, but where?
The bus outruns its headlights in the dark,
sucking diesel fuel.
I turn back to Joan of Arc,
where the French cause seems lost, too.
No one believes in her. But Joan insists:
"God speaks to me. I hear his voice."
"That's your imagination," they reply. "Of course,"
she says, "isn't that how God speaks?"

It's snow now—giddy, dizzy flakes
are multiplying everywhere.
They clean the air;
like once when I was lost in abstract
speculation, and a good friend asked:
"Can't we cut the crap
and just agree we're all together on this bus?"

At the service stop
we pile out—all of us
laughing. Woman in a burka holds her daughter up,
who points at the wildering white, amazed.
"Jesus, it's beautiful . . ."
a guy with a Rasta cap and dreadlocks says
as he catches a snowflake on his outstretched hand.
The year in its fairness comes round again.

IV

"The Garden Will Come to You" / A Conversation

Sit quietly. This is the only way.

—Frank X. Gaspar

I think of your little Buddha. We would welcome him
in our small backyard, though it might mean replacing
the plain stone bird, nestled by a broken brick,
next to the purple coneflowers and the rabble
of our almost-weeds. But wouldn't the Buddha say
"It's all the same: stone Buddha or stone bird.
Leave it as it is." I sit on my concrete stoop. I admire
the bird's stillness, its constancy. But I ask it
questions, too: There is the way of letting go, isn't there also
a way of embrace? The divine in each, in this one bird's
busy ribcage, in its ligaments and meat, risking itself
to the cat's pounce, to chance and our choices. God embodied
in the frantic wings, in the drifting—like "distracting snow"
　　　you say—
torn feathers of a mud brown dove. And yes, in the lithe cat, too,
not as a cruelty, but in its breath and agile bones, felt marrow
of its hungers and its glowing eye. *For I have perceived*
God's light about him, says Kit Smart, *both wax and fire*. It's folly
to take sides, but my wife has run some chicken-wire
fencing by our hemlock's overhanging fringe,
to slow the cats a bit. Something's at stake, though it's hard
to decipher the details. And so, we put no poisons on the grass.
　　　We planted
a tree out front, in the strip between our sidewalk and the street
where most of the neighbors have concrete. It grows without us

of course, drawing up water we can't see, floating its leaf fronds
    in the sun.
But we planted it—a blight-resistant elm, high as our attic now,
with a muscled trunk. I ask the sparrows, in its shadowed,
    interlacing leaves,
about these mysteries. All I pick up is a scattery, unmusical
cheep, cheep, cheep, the talk and tussle of their afternoon.
    Some call
and response, although I can't decipher it. They're fluttering
    unseen
in the shelter of the limbs that flute out like a beaker of
    champagne,
frothy in the spring, in full summer now, and generous
    with shade.

Yet Another Resurrection
Appearance

Now that she's gone
to live in another land
of deep attunements
and forgetfulness,
I'm bathing my mother
for the first time.

She sits, still
in sweatpants,
on a metal stool
in her shower stall.

I work downward
with an old, soft cloth,
cupping up warm water
with my other hand.

First, the knot of her neck;
then her back, a mottled brown;
the wing-like bones
of her shoulder blades.

Next I soap
the tender cup
of her clavicle.

Her breasts now—
almost gone, loose
and gently leathery.

So thin, her ribs
seem to count themselves
through her skin,
and the scar where they
made the incision
is smoother than a dime.

Now that I've laved
the silvery water
on her skin; touched
the bones of her wrists,
the hollows
of her palms; now
that I've set my hand
into the cusp
smooth beneath
each of her ghostly arms,
how could I not believe?

On Being Asked for a Poem That Embodies Non-Anthropocentric Spirituality

As a kid, I had a rock collection and didn't learn anything
from it. Not the scientific names. Not the way they formed
so long before us. Or the way they'll continue
eons after. I should, you say, have held them to my ear
hour after hour, and listened to their silence, to the pure
inhuman shape of them. But I'd have heard, instead,
the low, dark rumble of my blood. I kept them
in a box that I marked "stones," a box I got
from my father: thick pasteboard, with lots of gold gilt
edging the corners. You still could smell the cigars,
coronas they must have been, with a picture of peacocks
and a dark-haired woman on a gold divan. He travelled a lot
and I missed him dearly, and when he came back
he'd bring me a purple agate or, once, a plastic rocket
powered by a water pump. It never reached the stars,
the haze of coronas, the darkened dwarfs, the imponderable
empty spaces between them. It got about as high
as our maple tree. There's no getting round it. Whenever
I try to think of stones, all of the rest comes, too.

After Reading Amichai's Poem Called "Here," I Walk Past the Girls' Softball Practice

Scattering of fireflies
cool in evening air.
Green expanse of grass.

Fragile brown planet
of infield, glowing beyond
in shadowless ballfield light.

Lazy plink of bats.
All easy and genial:
ripple of laughter,
little rills of talk.

A slender blond girl
stretches in slow motion
to make a catch.

Which kind of beauty
is worth more? And what
kind of counting
would dare to ask?

Kant and His Manservant

Lampe is a pietist. He's also deeply
hungover. Still, after this morning's sermon—
first from his wife, then the one
about the Upper Room, how tongues of fire
raked the heads of the disciples
though none could see the flames
upon his own—he stumbles yet again
up the three back steps of Kant's dank home.

He watches the old man fumble for his spoon,
strain to eat a bit of roasted meat.
At precisely 4:00 p.m., Lampe
holds up the fraying empty arms
of Kant's wool coat and helps him pull it on.

The walks are shorter now
than forty years ago. Still they start
along the little linden alley, turn
just beyond the prison gate.
Kant grasps his Spanish stick
as always. These days though,
he oddly stamps each foot
a rigid perpendicular, believes
it gives him more resistance
so he won't fall down.
Yet fall he does, when he's alone.

Kant rambles on: The eighty-seven cats
that died in Brandenburg are gone
because cats' bodies are "electrical."
If Prussian candles weren't impure
his nightcap wouldn't keep on catching fire.
"Beer is poisonous." His servant's heard it all.

They turn for home. They creep along
at Kant's excruciating pace. The winter light
is blurring into indigo again.

Lampe's ruined head still burns. It's all
his tongue can do to move, make sound.
The dimming street is smoking with fresh dung.
"Sir, let me help you round. . . ." His aged arm
takes on Kant's weight as if it were his own.

Pluto 3

I'm making my usual orbit through the neighborhood:
Pock-marked surface of the sidewalk aggregate. Unexpected flare
of tulips in a weedy lot. Motions of the residents: girl I've never seen,
with headphones, lost in some music of the spheres. Mr. Washington,
thick-rimmed glasses on, coming through his chain-link gate,
followed by his baggy-trousered, sulking son. No one disputes
Copernicus—his diagram of circles, epicycles, equants
no more elegant than Ptolemy's. No one disputes Kepler—
astrologer and mystical Pythagorean, who got ellipses right.
But Tombaugh, poor Clyde Tombaugh, that's a different
order of magnitude. Surely we'd have found Pluto
without him. Then, too, he'd seen those UFOs.
Still, you've got to love him, for the lonely years of nights
poring at his photographic plates. No one argues, either,
for my neighbor Rege, who sets up a barrel telescope
on his front stoop, rarely seeing much in the litter of our city lights.
No one argues for the Lady with Three Dogs, down to
one dog now, a wavering dingy moon she carries half the time.
I'm back to the rental block, a dimming galaxy of dandelion puffs
floating at its unmowed front. Arc of a bus that leans around a corner
trailing plumed exhaust. Boy on his bike, late to get home,
as dusk and the headlights start to come. Streetlamps now.
Couples with ice cream cones. Glitter of broken glass.

The Turning

This is the turning where the fruit once was. She knows it
in her slender bones. Here, at the meadow's edge,
windfall and strewn, among the soft grasses and goldenrod.
She moves so easily along the path, opened long ago
by her own slim shoulders and her tawny belly-sway.
She is perfectly herself, as she passes through
a curtain-edge of birch and evergreens, and slips away.

He comes after, half his rack of antlers gone,
scenting and hesitant, as if that lovely,
shaggy-gray ghost of tree might still be there.
As if he could taste those gnarled, green apples
even now, but couldn't yet decide if they had been
a bitter kind of knowing or the very thing
that nourished and sustained him all these years.

All Hallows' Eve

Then, ahead of me, he was immersed in the fire,
asking Statius, who for a long way now
had walked between us, to come through last.
—Purgatorio XXVII, 46–48

There we go, good friends, a straggly line
past the fake fences and plastic tombstones,
real enough to us, cloaked in our dreamed-of selves—
astronaut, ballerina, cardboard-headed lion—
up the steep steps, across the flickering thresholds
into a foreign light. We clutch our pillowcases
by the hems and hold them out. We hurry.
We laugh, despite the wintry air, a sharp
black fire that crackles like static between us.
We coax each other on, along the broken sidewalks, shying
at shadows, through the skeletal rattle of the leaves.
There we go. Goodbye. And thanks.

Elegy with Braids and Tulips

for Melvin Jordan, 1941–2006

In what I tell you, there's the almost-true, the sometimes-true,
and the half-true. That's what telling a life is like, braiding all of
that like one plaits the white Indies currant's hair to make a hut.
And the true-true comes out of that braid. And Sophie, you can't
be scared of lying if you want to know everything . . .
     —Patrick Chamoiseau, from his novel *Texaco*

The Dow fell 4 percent again. More night raids
in Afghanistan. It starts that joke you'd always run:
I heard about it. I'd reply: *And I was horrified.*
Applicable to everything: Your mother lost her keys
down the toilet. You were out of smokes.
You're gone. I'm turning 55, the time
when more and more these absences begin
braiding into the ordinary.
                              The time you sang
the *Lux Aeterna*, Rutter's *Requiem*. The turning shape
of your brown hands, thumbing the dog-eared pages
of your Dostoyevsky, who made his Sonia read
from John, the part on Lazarus. But let's not kid ourselves
with any Band of Angels, twinkling of an eye, the body
incorruptible. So, what could Dostoyevsky mean
by writing that, if forced, he'd choose
not "Truth" but "Christ?"
                              Hard rain this afternoon.
Lots of downed leaves, yellow, yellow-brown,
pasted like stars on the sidewalks, bunched along
the bottom of each chain-link fence. Now,

a few torn clouds across the skyline, as dusk
weaves imperceptibly to dark.
                                    I'm waiting for a bus—
no destination, just a need to ride. *Eternity's in love*
with the productions of time, says Blake.
Beneath the buzzing of fluorescent lights
it's just the driver and a few of us. Two kids
with orange hair and arm tattoos. Your ghost appears:
you cock your head aside and whisper, *Heard about it.*
I was horrified. There's dust on your shoes
and star-like flecks of spackling on your jeans. Strange
since you'd been trained in opera, not construction.
I see you've got the shakes again.
                                    A woman,
in the seat across, plaits her daughter's hair.
The child sleeps. Outside the smeared bus window,
city traffic hustles by. The moon is running
in the gusty sky. *Time is the poetry of eternity.*
Eternity's in love with lies. Eternity's in love
with incarnation. Incarnation's an embrace
that's not afraid to die.
                                    I pull out a wallet photo—
the only one I have of you: beyond
your blue-tweed sport coat, easy
outspread arms, your laugh, your close-cut beard,
behind a coffee pot and stack of plastic cups,
we see some yellow tulips—out of focus,
slightly cropped. The photograph a lie
of course, because it's autumn now, and yet
not quite, since one of the yellow heads

is slumping visibly and tinged with brown. *Eternity's*
in love with the productions of time, beautiful
and blurred behind you.

End of the line.

I watch the woman and her child get off.
There's one spot of neon in the dark commercial block.
The daughter waits. Her tired head droops.
Her mom picks up their grocery bags again
and weaves her fingers in the girl's loose hand.

I heard about it, Melvin, and I held it close.

Each Perfected Name

And they realized that the end was still far, far away, and that
the hardest, the most complicated part was only just beginning.
          —Anton Chekhov, "The Lady with the Dog"

Was it the 9th or 10th? There was no notice of her death
in the city papers, just a snowy hush across our neighborhood,
broken by the scrape of shovels. We stood
half bowed, to get our breath. Almost Christmas, yes,
but all we knew was that the sidewalks turned to slush,
then a ghostly fog, and Helen wasn't walking with her dog.

Whatever day it was, her final breaths were in an ambulance,
being moved from Mercy into hospice care.
A boyish EMT brushed a sweat-damp wisp of hair
from off her forehead, held a penlight to her eye.

People asked about her at the corner, on the bus.
A neighbor took her dog. But for weeks
her body waited—sheeted, washed, and brushed,
but unattended—at the County Morgue.

              * * *

Helen, our Holy Fool,
leaving stale breadcrusts for the pigeons and the jays.
Giant Eagle, CoGo's, St. Rosalia School;
Greenfield, Windsor, Mirror, every blessèd street
and alleyway—every weather, every time of day.

When we first met, I'd greet her with a word—
she barely spoke. Lost in her overcoat,
she'd back away, skittery and small:
"You're a good man, sir . . . yes sir . . . yes sir."

Over the years, though, different:
Her skirts still out-of-date and frayed,
her hair unkempt, yet she displayed
an undeniable bent for fashion:
just the right hint of midnight blue or mauve
in both her scarf and blouse.

Or, without quite seeing it, we'd sense
that one of her trinity of dogs was absent
from the turbulence and tangle of her leash.
Then, another year, another gone,
disappearing quietly, like griefs.

* * *

Our talks grew longer:
"Where will you be goin' on vacation?"
"Maine, again." "And will ya' be stayin'
near the Kennedys, with all those rich?"
Or: "You're so educated." "How you dress!"

She told me once that kids would call her "crone";
that someone once had thrown a beer can at her
from a passing car. It was two days into Lent:
I still could see the ghost of ash
upon her forehead like a mark of caste.

I picture how she must have been at Mass,
taking the wafer on her tongue.
Hospital, hospice, host—her single self.
Candle in a small red glass
that flickers on an icon shelf.

* * *

February now. Things long hidden start to show:
brown patches in the backyards, scattered trash,
our sidewalks etched with salt and grit. Then,
in the evenings, you begin to notice it—light
hangs longer in the sky. Through the tangled phone lines
as you crest a hill, you catch a startling rose and yellow glow.

Getting coffee at a place I frequent,
but a little far from home, I mentioned feeling glum
at having lost a friend. "A woman who was always with her dog,"
I said, "a local character." A glimpse of recognition
in the server's face: "You knew her, too?" I asked.
"No, but a woman who was here just mentioned her. . . ."

* * *

Being of great but unsound heart, and of a mind
of odd, uncertain parts, Helen R. Lavelle,
in her unwritten testament and will, bequeaths
this catalogue: Item: prepaid sublease
on brown, frame house with porch that sags.
Item: aging, dingy dog. Item: on the porch,
her last effects, a mound of plastic garbage bags.

Filled with what—who knows?
Three frayed leashes, each metal clasp a question mark,
dresser-and-a-closet's-worth of clothes,
weathered high-top shoes, a kitchen clock,
transistor radio, a sparse but matching set
of boneware dishes, pasteboard box of hair barrettes.

Intangible bequests to all the neighborhood:
Her crazy affirmations, compliments.
Wide, erratic circles, her unceasing steps.

* * *

Gathered to remember her, we sit, a quiet cluster
at the rear of St. Rosalia's. Tonight, the "little saint"
is cloaked in violet for Lent. Most of us non-Catholic,
unsure of ritual and prayer, we cannot take the sacrament.

Still, we shuffle forward, kneel. The unfamiliar ash
is rough upon our skin. Mixed with it, a sheen
of oil: a fingerprint, a seal, a ghostly claim. And maybe,
there, the glistening of each perfected name.

* * *

Outside, it's cold, and yet we linger on the steps.
Partly out of friendliness. Partly cause it's dark;
we like the glow of porch-light. Partly,
it's because we sense that when we go—
marked with the gritty ash and fingerprints—
that when we pass McNally's, Yesterday's,

the Win-Green Bar, and Tanya's Beauty (where
"we specialize in every kind of hair"),
past the closed consignment store, its dusty windows,
armless mannequins, past the faded crosswalks
that don't protect from anything, past
the street kids hanging by the park, back to the circles
of our homes and work, that's when
the hardest, the most complicated part begins.

About the Author

Richard St. John's first book of poems, *The Pure Inconstancy of Grace*, was published in 2005 by Truman State University Press, as first runner-up for the 2004 T. S. Eliot Prize for Poetry. His long poem *Shrine* was released as a chapbook in 2011. His work has also appeared in *Sewanee Review, Poet Lore,* and *Chautauqua,* as well as many other periodicals and anthologies.

St. John received degrees in English from Princeton University and the University of Virginia. In 2002, he completed a mid-career Loeb Fellowship at Harvard University. He lives in Pittsburgh, Pennsylvania, with his wife, Kate.

He has read widely across the country, connecting not only with university and literary audiences, but also with listeners new to poetry.

For more information, please visit www.richardstjohnpoet.com.